# EARTHWISE

# Water

## Jim Pipe

### Franklin Watts
### London • Sydney

# CONTENTS

© Aladdin Books Ltd 2004

Designed and produced by
Aladdin Books Ltd
28 Percy Street
London W1T 2BZ

First published in
Great Britain in 2004 by
Franklin Watts
96 Leonard Street
London EC2A 4XD

ISBN 0 7496 5396 5

Design
Flick, Book Design
and Graphics

Educational Consultant
Jackie Holderness

Picture research
Brian Hunter Smart

A catalogue record for
this book is available
from the British Library.

Printed in UAE

# INTRODUCTION

Everyone needs water! Farmers need it
for growing food and factories need it to
do their work. No animal or plant could
survive without it. This book explains
why water is so precious, where it
comes from, and why we need to save it.

### HOW TO USE THIS BOOK

Look for the symbol
of the magnifying glass
for seasonal observation
tips and ideas.

The paintbrush
boxes contain an activity
you can do that is related
to a specific season.

# OUR BLUE PLANET

From space, the Earth looks blue. That's because water covers more than two-thirds of our planet's surface. It fills our oceans, rivers, lakes and reservoirs. Frozen into giant sheets of ice, water covers both poles of our planet. It is also in the air we breathe. Water is all around us.

Salt water in the sea

Fresh water in rivers

Polar ice is frozen water

Give yourself a pinch; you may feel fairly solid but in fact you're 67 per cent water (the same as a mouse). All animals and plants are mostly made up of water – a potato is about 80 per cent water.

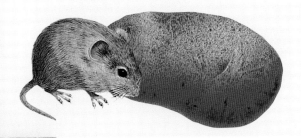

Although billions of tonnes of water fill the oceans, this water is too salty to drink and cannot be used on farms or in most factories. By comparison, only a small amount of the world's water is fresh (unsalty). But most of this water is frozen solid as ice at the poles, or is in the ground.

# Water Words

Water looks, sounds and feels like nothing else. Think of some words which could be used to describe water. Then try to write a story or a poem about it. You could think about how it feels when you take a bath or go for a swim. Or imagine the noises water can make, such as bubbling, gurgling and splashing.

splosh

float

spray

ripple

clear

wet

blue

plop!

cool

# WATER FOR LIFE

Your body cannot work without water. In fact, you need a constant supply of water to stay alive. When you get thirsty, your body is asking for more water!

Like other animals, you get water from drinking and eating. Plants get water from rain or they suck it up from the ground through their roots.

To stay healthy, you should drink about 2 litres of water every day. People can live for weeks without food, but we can only survive for a few days without water.

**Zebras drinking from a river**

# Water Stores

Camels can survive for weeks without any water. This is why they are used to carry food and people on long desert journeys. They can store up to 5 litres of water in their stomachs, and unlike most animals they can quench their thirst with salt water. Find out more about these amazing animals using the internet (right), a CD-ROM or books.

## PRICKLY • PLANTS

Have you seen a cactus? These desert plants can survive for a long time without water, because they can store water in their thick stems. If you have a cactus at home you hardly need to water it. Does your cactus have prickles? These help to protect it from thirsty animals!

Plants take in water from the soil through tiny hairs on their roots. The water travels up the stem and into the plant's leaves. Water also keeps a plant's stem rigid. Without water, it soon droops!

Flower

Leaves

Stem

Roots

# FRESH WATER

We don't only drink fresh water. We use huge amounts of it every day: for cleaning, cooking, washing clothes and dishes, brushing our teeth, carrying away waste, watering the garden and filling pools (left) and ponds.

# Water in the Home

Each of us uses about 250 litres of water every day. Flushing the toilet uses the most water in the home, followed closely by showers and baths. Can you draw a picture showing how you and your family use water in each room (don't forget the garden)?

Each time you flush a toilet, it uses 15 litres of water.

It takes more than 30 litres to wash a day's dishes by hand.

A ten-minute car wash with a hose can use over 100 litres of water!

# **S** QUELCH!

We also get water from the food we eat. Juicy fruits like tomatoes and oranges are around 90 per cent water, while a loaf of bread is 30 per cent water. Can you think of any food without much water in it?

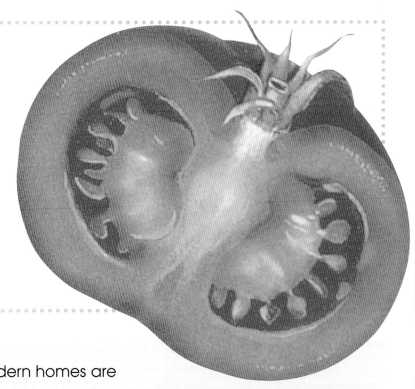

A full bath uses over 150 litres of water.

It takes about 150 litres to run a washing machine.

Most modern homes are connected to a public water system that supplies all their water, so that if you want a drink you simply turn on a tap.

However, millions of homes around the world have no running water and even then it may not be safe to drink. Some families have to pump water by hand from a well, or collect it in jars from local rivers.

# WATER AT WORK

Fresh water is used in many factories for cooling machines down or cleaning, though power stations and some factories use salt water instead.

Large quantities of water are used in the production of metal (below), wood and paper products, chemicals and oils.

Most of the world's fresh water supplies are used for growing the crops that feed us. Some crops need more water than others – rice only grows in fields that are constantly flooded, called paddies (left).

Some farmers channel the water from rivers using a system of canals, ditches or plastic pipes. They also pump up water trapped in the ground, using giant sprinklers to throw water over a large area.

# WATER • WASTERS

Does anyone you know use a sprinkler to water their garden? Garden sprinklers use a lot of water – a powerful one will use as much as 800 litres in an hour! A lot of this water evaporates or blows away before it hits the ground. But a lot less water is needed if you use a watering can.

Thirsty cows, sheep, pigs and chickens need fresh water, too. A cow that produces milk drinks about 60 litres a day, while a pig drinks about 15 litres of water a day.

Not surprisingly, a lot of water is also needed to farm freshwater fish such as trout.

# THE WATER CYCLE

A cycle means something that goes round and round, and that's exactly what happens to the water on Earth. The Sun warms water in the sea, turning it into a gas which rises up into the sky. Here the gas turns back into water, which falls to the ground as rain. The rain flows in rivers down to the sea, where the Sun warms it and turns it into a gas again!

The water cycle means that the water on our planet gets used over and over again.

So, the raindrops falling on your head today, contain the same water that fell on the dinosaurs millions of years ago!

# VANISHING PUDDLES

Have you ever noticed how a puddle vanishes into thin air (above)? The Sun's heat turns water into an invisible gas called water vapour. This rises up into the air, like the steam from a kettle. We say that it 'evaporates' into the air.

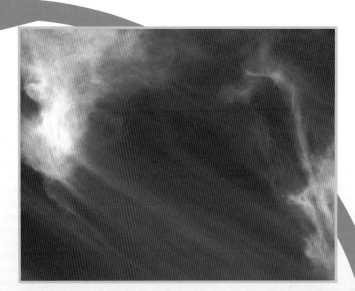

**1** Heat from the Sun turns water on the surface of seas and lakes into a gas called water vapour.

**2** The water vapour rises into the air. Here it cools down and forms clouds of water droplets.

**4** The rain flows into streams and rivers which flow into the seas, lakes and ponds. Then the cycle begins all over again!

**3** Slowly, the water droplets get bigger and heavier until they are so heavy that they fall to the ground as raindrops.

## RAINY DAYS

Whether it drizzles or pours, rain provides us with much of our fresh water. On a rainy day, notice how most of the water runs away or soaks into the ground.

Scientists use centimetres to describe how much rain has fallen. For example, three centimetres of rain doesn't sound like a lot, but falling over a whole city it adds up to billions of litres of water!

## A Waterproof Coat

Our skin is almost completely waterproof. Drop water from a straw onto your bare arm and the drops just trickle away (right). Now make a collection of all the coats, jackets, hats and umbrellas you have. Use a wet sponge to test them. The most waterproof coats are the ones where no water soaks into the material.

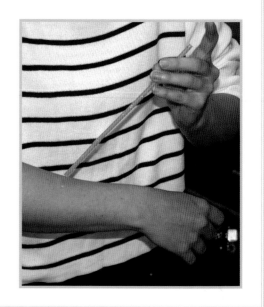

Rainwater that soaks into the ground trickles down into spaces between rocks or grains of sand. Some types of rock, called aquifers, store enormous amounts of water.

By drilling down, we can pump this water to the surface. Underground water can also bubble up to the surface on its own, creating a well or a spring.

Most animals have a waterproof coat. Flamingoes (above) and other birds cover their feathers with oil from their body. Water slides off the oily feathers. Sheep also have oil in their woolly coats that stops the water soaking in.

## WRINKLY • SKIN

Next time you take a long bath, look at your skin after you get out. It will probably be all wrinkly. That's because the oil that is naturally in your skin, and makes it waterproof, has been washed off.

# FLOODS AND DROUGHTS

Rain can have a big effect on our lives. In some tropical countries it pours for months on end during the wet season. These heavy rains, called the monsoon, often bring severe floods that can ruin crops and make many people homeless.

In other regions it may not rain for months, causing a drought that can also destroy crops and make life hard for animals and people.

## FLOOD • DANGER

Have you ever seen a flood? Streets and fields are covered in water and many houses are badly damaged. People have to be very careful where they walk or drive as the water can be very deep. Some people have to use a boat to escape.

A desert (right) is an extremely dry region that is often very hot. It receives very little rain, and in some cases, all the rain falls in one or two huge showers. Only very tough plants, such as a cactus, can live in a desert. But where water springs up from below the ground, it forms an oasis, an area where crops can grow.

# Wet or Dry?

Look at a map of the world which shows the Earth's features. Try to find areas that get very little rain, such as deserts or the poles, and areas that get a lot of rain, such as rainforests. Then copy a world map and mark on it rainy areas in blue and dry areas in yellow.

In a very bad drought the soil becomes dry and cracked (below) and the lack of rain causes farm crops to wither and die. Streams, ponds and wells may dry up and animals may die from lack of water. Forest fires are also common because of the dry conditions.

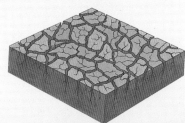

A dam is a barrier across a river that stops the water flowing. A lake forms behind the dam, creating a large store of water for dry seasons, or for watering crops.

# FLOWING WATER

When rain falls, it doesn't just sit there! Most flows downhill, filling rivers and lakes as well as shaping the land by moving rocks or soil. Over thousands of years, flowing water can carve out valleys and wear down mountains.

In streams and rivers high up in the mountains, water often flows fast. When a river reaches flatter, low-lying areas, it flows gently towards the sea.

Rafting on a fast-flowing mountain river

When water flows over a rock, part of the rock mixes into the water, or dissolves. When this happens in a cave, the water leaves behind a tiny piece of rock as it evaporates.

Over thousands of years, millions of tiny pieces build up into strange shapes called stalactites (on the cave roof) and stalagmites (on the floor).

Flowing water has enormous power. People once used this power in mills. Water from a stream rushed over a large waterwheel, making it turn. This was connected to a heavy stone which ground corn into flour.

Today, we also use the power of falling water in dams and waterfalls to make electricity.

## DISSOLVE

Have you noticed how a lump of sugar (below) quickly dissolves in hot water? Warm water inside you helps you to dissolve food in the same way, then helps to carry nutrients around your body.

# GOOD ENOUGH TO DRINK

All of the water that we use in our homes comes from either a store in the ground, such as a well, or from a river, lake or reservoir.

Before it comes into our homes, the water is cleaned. It is passed through a filter to remove mud and bacteria, then chemicals such as chlorine are added to kill any dangerous germs. Other chemicals are added to improve its taste or smell.

## The Taste Test

Does water always taste the same? Pour tap water, soda water and mineral water into glasses. Then take a sip from each one. Although the three waters all look the same, each one contains different chemicals that probably make them taste slightly different.

That's why you should be careful about the water you drink. Even if water in a stream looks clean, you can't see what's really in it!

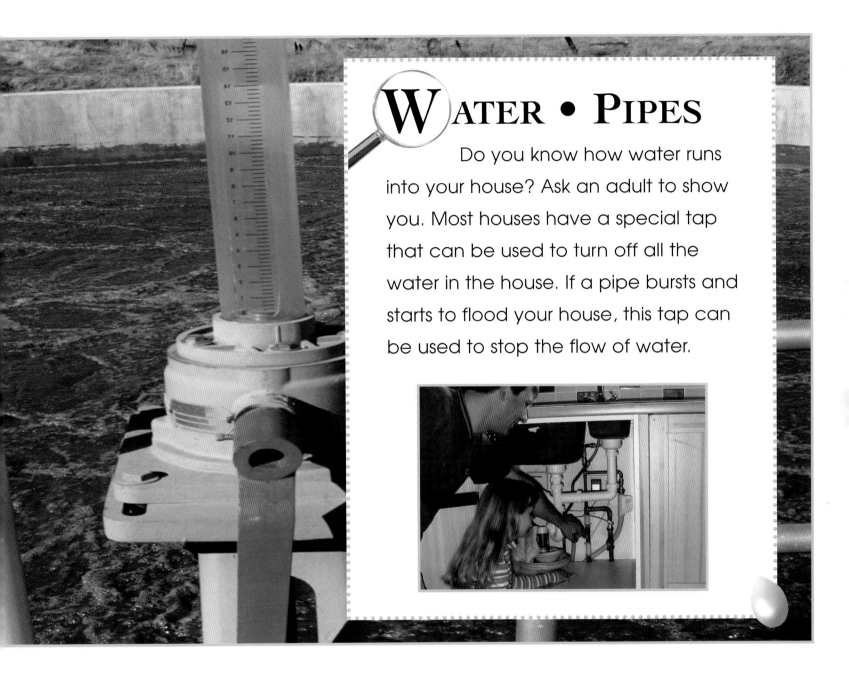

# Water • Pipes

Do you know how water runs into your house? Ask an adult to show you. Most houses have a special tap that can be used to turn off all the water in the house. If a pipe bursts and starts to flood your house, this tap can be used to stop the flow of water.

The cleaned water is pumped into large pipes called water mains. These are buried beneath the streets. They connect with smaller pipes that lead to every home, office and factory. A pumping station creates the pressure that pushes the water along the pipes. Water is then carried around your home by copper or plastic pipes. So water that pours from your tap has already come a long way!

# DIRTY WATER

Many of the ways we use water make it dirty, such as having a bath, washing our clothes, or using the toilet. Often we use soap, washing-up liquid, shampoo and washing powder. All of these contain chemicals, called detergents, which help to wash off the dirt.

We use a lot of water to carry away wastes from the toilet or kitchen. This water, and the waste it carries, is called sewage. Another system of pipes under the streets carries sewage away from homes and offices. This is called a sewer system.

Detergents work by making oily dirt and water stick together. But when we have finished washing, the chemicals in the detergent go down the drain along with the water and dirt. This pollutes the water.

Sometimes detergents from homes or factories go straight into rivers, polluting the fresh water with foam or slime that can kill plants and animals.

# CLEAN & GENTLE

Some washing-up liquids and shampoos have chemicals in them that are less harmful to nature and make the water easier to clean. These are called biodegradable chemicals. When you go shopping, try to spot some of these environmentally-friendly products.

# WATER POLLUTION

Water may also be polluted by chemicals from factories spilling into nearby rivers and lakes, or by chemicals that farmers use to help their plants grow or to protect crops from insects.

When crops are sprayed, some of the chemicals go into the soil. From there, they get into streams and rivers or into water that is in the ground.

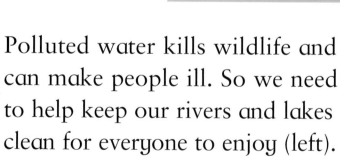

Polluted water kills wildlife and can make people ill. So we need to help keep our rivers and lakes clean for everyone to enjoy (left).

If you have a garden, try to use environmentally-friendly bug sprays and fertilisers. Also, make sure you dispose of your litter carefully, especially items such as batteries and glues which have harmful chemicals in them.

Cars and factories also pollute the air (below). This pollution mixes with water in the air, making the water more acidic. When acid rain falls, it pollutes lakes, rivers, seas and the ground, killing fish, frogs and other animals and damaging trees (left).

# GREEN • CLEAN

Have you ever noticed the green slime that floats on ponds? This mass of tiny creatures, called algae, actually helps to clean the water. Waste in the pond feeds the algae, which in turn feeds fish and other pond animals. But when ponds get polluted, the algae grows too fast, making it hard for anything else to live in the water.

# SAVING WATER

The water that is here on Earth now is all the water that we will ever have. So we should look after it. It's easy to waste water, but everyone can help. Remember, just leaving a tap dripping overnight can waste more than two litres of water!

A single drip doesn't waste much water – but the water lost from a leaky pipe soon adds up. If it leaks 1 litre of water every 10 minutes, that means that you are losing over 140 litres a day, or over 50,000 litres a year. That's enough for almost 350 baths!

# Save It!

Here are some things we can all do to help make sure that there will always be water for everyone:

- Turn off dripping taps.
- Take showers instead of baths.
- Use rainwater to water the plants rather than tap water.
- Turn off the tap while washing, brushing teeth or washing dishes.
- Don't run the dishwasher unless it is full. Wash up by hand instead.
- Don't use the toilet as a waste basket – every flush uses 15 litres of water.

Can you make a poster to encourage your friends to help?

# WONDER WATER

At first sight, water doesn't seem very interesting – it has no colour, no taste and no smell. But think of what it can do. It keeps us alive, helps our food to grow, and keeps us clean. It can also be a lot of fun! That's why we need to be careful how we use it, so there is plenty for everyone, now and in the future.

Many ancient peoples believed that rain was created by a god or gods. So in times of drought or flood, they prayed to their gods and made offerings to them.

Today, many cultures around the world still hold water festivals celebrating the wonder of water!

For fun

To drink

For growing food

As a home

Can you think of any other ways water is used?

# WATERWAYS

If you look on a map, you will see that many towns are near rivers. That's because as well as supplying fresh water, rivers were one of the fastest ways to get about before there were trains or cars.

Canals and rivers are still used by boats to move goods around, as well as being a fun place to spend a holiday (below)!

Across the world, rivers (below) are the source of most of the fresh water we use. As the number of people in the world continues to grow, we must find new sources of fresh water, or find cheaper ways to turn salt water from the sea into fresh water that we can drink.

# USEFUL WORDS

**acid rain** – rain that is very acidic, usually due to air pollution.

**biodegradable** – able to be broken down by bacteria.

**dam** – a wall built to hold back the water of a stream or river.

**detergent** – chemicals for cleaning that act like soap.

**dissolve** – to make something liquid, often by putting it into liquid.

**drought** – a long period of dry and often very hot weather.

**environmentally-friendly** – products that are biodegradable or less harmful to the environment.

**evaporate** – to change from a liquid to a vapour or gas.

**fertiliser** – substances that are put into the soil to help plants grow.

**oasis** – a place in the desert where there are water springs in the ground.

**ocean** – the great body of water that covers more than 70 per cent of the Earth's surface.

**reservoir** – a place where water is collected and stored for use, often in a lake behind a dam.

**spring** – a stream of water flowing from the ground.

**stalactite** – a rock formation that hangs like an icicle from the roof of a cave.

**stalagmite** – a rock formation shaped like a cone on the floor of a cave. Like a stalactite, it is formed by dripping water.

**water cycle** – the natural cycle in which water evaporates from seas and lakes, forms clouds then returns to the ground as rain.

**waterproof** – a material that does not let water through.

# Find Out More

If you want to find out more, take a look at these books and websites:

**Books:** I Can Help Save Water (Franklin Watts); A Drop of Water (Scholastic Press); Focus on Water (Franklin Watts).

**Websites:** www.savewater.com.au
www.environment-agency.gov.uk/kids
www.floridaswater.com

# WATER WATCH

Can you find out where the water in your hometown comes from? While smaller towns usually have a local supply, bigger cities may have water pumped from reservoirs far away. There may be a reservoir near you, especially if you live in a hilly or mountainous region. Take a look at a map of your area.

# INDEX

**Photocredits**
Abbreviations: l-left, r-right, b-bottom, t-top, c-centre, m-middle, ba-background
Front cover tr & br, 1, 5br, 6b, 8tl, 13tl, 15mr, 18b — Digital Stock. Front cover tl, back cover, 4t, 4br, 9ml, 13tr, 13bl, 16-17,
17bm, 27br, 28ml, 28bmr, 30mr — Corbis. Front cover bl, 18ml, 21tl, 23tl, 23br, 25mr, 25br, 30-31 — Photodisc. Front cover
inset, 6tr, 7tr, 8mr, 8bl, 8br, 9bl, 11bm, 12tr, 14br, 19br, 21mr, 23tr, 27bl, 28bml, 31bl — Flick Smith. Front cover c, 3c, 4bm,
20tl, 24bl, 26tr, 27bm, 28bl, 32b — Comstock. 2-3, 4bl, 13br — Stockbyte. 9br, 17tr, 19tl, 28c, 28br, 29 both — Corel. 10b, 11t
— Flat Earth. 11br, 14tr — Select. 15bm — Roger Vlitos. 16br, 22b — Corbis Royalty Free. 24c — John Deere. 25tl — Will &
Deni McIntyre/CORBIS. 26b — Digital Vision. 27tr — Brand X Pictures.